SPORTS MATH

Math and My World

Kieran Walsh

Rourke
Publishing LLC
Vero Beach, Florida 32964

© 2006 Rourke Publishing LLC

All rights reserved. No part of this book may be reproduced or utilized in any form or by any means, electronic or mechanical including photocopying, recording, or by any information storage and retrieval system without permission in writing from the publisher.

www.rourkepublishing.com

PHOTO CREDITS:
All photos from AbleStock.com, except for page 6 by the author

Editor: Frank Sloan

Library of Congress Cataloging-in-Publication Data

Walsh, Kieran.
  Sports math / Kieran Walsh.
      p. cm. -- (Math and my world II)
  Includes index.
  ISBN 1-59515-495-7 (hardcover)
  1. Arithmetic--Juvenile literature. 2. Sports--Juvenile literature. I.
Title II. Series: Walsh, Kieran. Math and my world II.

  QA115.W276 2006
  513--dc22
                                        2005015008

Printed in the USA

w/w

TABLE OF CONTENTS

INTRODUCTION

Think about math and sports. How do they relate? What does one have to do with the other?

Sports and math have everything to do with one another. For instance, how many points is the winning team winning by?

Well, for one thing, mathematics plays a large part in how winning is determined. If, at the end of a hockey game, the winning team has a score of 7 and the losing team has a score of 4, how many points did the winning team win by?

Finding the answer is simple. Just subtract the smaller number from the larger number:

$$7 - 4 = 3$$

The winning team won by 3 points!

In terms of the relationship between math and sports, though, scores are just the tip of the iceberg. In fact, it wouldn't be unreasonable to say that sports are pure math. Mathematics in motion!

Read on and find out for yourself!

BASEBALL

It is believed that the first game of modern baseball was played in 1845 in Hoboken, New Jersey. Using that date as a starting point, can you figure out how old baseball is?

Cooperstown, New York is the location of Doubleday Field and The National Baseball Hall of Fame.

The answer depends on when you are reading this book. However, let's assume that the current year is 2006. Now all you have to do to find the answer is to subtract the smaller number from the larger number:

$$2006 - 1845 = 161$$

Baseball is about 161 years old!

In 1858, a man named Henry Chadwick wrote the rule book for baseball. The rules Chadwick recorded have changed slightly over the years, but the game of baseball is still very much the same as it was in the 19th century. Let's take a look at how a baseball game works.

In a baseball game, there are two teams. These teams take turns playing **offense** and **defense**. The team playing defense has 9 players on the field in the following postitions: pitcher, catcher, first baseman, second baseman, third baseman, shortstop, right field, center field, left field.

Meanwhile, the team playing offense sends batters to home plate. These batters attempt to hit the balls thrown by the pitcher to the catcher. The distance from the pitcher's mound to home plate is 60.5 feet.

Professional pitchers are capable of throwing a baseball at incredible speeds. Much of the time, these pitches reach velocities of over 90 miles per hour! If a baseball is traveling at 90 mph, how long does it take to travel 60.5 feet?

If this boy delivers a pitch that travels at 60 miles ▶
per hour, how quickly will it reach the batter?

First of all, it is important to understand that we are comparing a very large quantity (the speed of the ball) to a much smaller quantity (the distance from the pitcher's mound to home plate). In order to calculate a sensible answer, you're going to have to convert some numbers.

In one mile, there are 5,280 feet. How many feet are there in 90 miles?

$$90 \times 5{,}280 = 475{,}200$$

So a baseball traveling at 90 mph is traveling at 475,200 *feet* per hour!

Baseballs travel at incredible speeds and can be dangerous, so the catcher always wears a protective mask and catches with a mitt.

As you can imagine, a baseball traveling at that speed won't take very long to reach the catcher's mitt. In fact, it's pointless to talk about it in terms of a measurement *per hour*. Rather, a baseball traveling at that speed will reach home plate in a matter of seconds.

How many seconds are there in one hour? There are 60 minutes in an hour, and 60 seconds per minute, so:

$$60 \times 60 = 3600$$

There are 3,600 seconds in one hour!

If a baseball is traveling at 475,200 feet per hour, how many feet is it covering per second? You can find out by dividing the speed of the baseball per hour by the number of seconds in an hour:

$$475{,}200 \div 3600 = 132$$

The baseball is traveling at a speed of 132 feet per second! How long will it take a ball traveling at that speed to go the 60.5 feet distance from the pitcher's mound to home plate?

You can find out by dividing the distance by the speed:

$$60.5 \div 132 = 0.4583$$

A ball thrown at 90 mph reaches home plate in less than half a second! This is something to bear in mind when considering a player's batting average.

If this boy ends the season with 400 at-bats and 57 hits, what is his batting average?

Batting averages are determined using two numbers. The first is the number of times at-bat, or the number of chances a player has to hit a ball. The second number is the number of actual hits a player gets.

Consider an imaginary player who has 623 at-bats and 178 hits. What would his batting average be?

To find out, you need to divide the number of hits by the number of at-bats:

$$178 \div 623 = .285$$

The imaginary player's batting average is .285! But is that good or bad?

In terms of batting average, anything over .270 is considered good, while an average over .300 is great. Anything over .330 is incredible. So, our imaginary player has a pretty good average.

Another way to think about this is to consider the batting average in terms of percentage. A batting average is really a number that tells what percentage of balls a player has actually managed to hit.

Take the imaginary player again. How can you convert his batting average, .285, to a percentage?

It's easy. Just multiply it by 100:

$$.285 \times 100 = 28.5$$

28.5 percent! That wouldn't be a very good test score, but it's considered good for a batter. That gives you some idea of just how hard it is to hit a baseball coming at you at 90 mph!

Home Run Kings

For forty years, the baseball player responsible for hitting the most home runs in a single season was Roger Maris. In 1961, Maris hit a total of 61 home runs, narrowly outdoing the previous record of 60 set by Babe Ruth. In 1998, this record was beaten twice by Mark McGwire and Sammy Sosa of the Chicago Cubs. Their totals were, respectively, 70 home runs for McGwire and 66 for Sosa. The current record, though, is held by Barry Bonds, who in 2001 managed 73 home runs!

How many more home runs did Barry Bonds get than Roger Maris?

$$73 - 61 = 12$$

Bonds got 12 more home runs than Maris!

FOOTBALL

Baseball is unique in that it is played on a diamond-shaped field. Most sports, including soccer, hockey, and lacrosse, are played on rectangular fields. Probably the most popular sport played on a rectangular field is football.

Including the end zones, an entire football field is 120 yards long. How long is half of a football field including the end zone?

Without counting the end zones, which take up a space of 10 yards each, a professional football field is exactly 100 yards long. Football fields are labeled with a series of yard lines. At the exact center of the football field is the 50-yard line. Remember that a football field is 100 yards long. How do those two numbers relate?

50   100

50 is exactly *half* of 100. You can see this for yourself by multiplying 50 by 2:

50 x 2 = 100

This is an important point to make in terms of understanding how football is played. A football field is really kind of like two separate fields stuck together. The team with possession of the ball, (the offense) tries to invade the defending team's field and eventually cross their goal line to score a touchdown. Starting from the 50-yard line, a team on the offensive has to push forward 50 yards to get a touchdown.

The defense, though, tries to prevent the offensive team from gaining any yardage by pushing the **line of scrimmage** back. The line of scrimmage is a set of imaginary lines that determine where players will line up before the next play, and its location is determined by where the last play ended.

For instance, what if the defense manages to push the offensive line from the 50-yard line to the 30-yard line? How many yards does the offense now have to cover to make a touchdown?

First of all, you have to find out how many yards away from the 50-yard line the offense is. You can do this by subtracting the team's current location (the 30-yard line) from 50:

$$50 - 30 = 20$$

The offense team is 20 yards from the 50-yard line!

Now add the two remaining distances together:

$$50 + 20 = 70$$

To make a touchdown, the offense team has to cover 70 yards!

The team that has possession of the ball is given just 4 downs, or plays, to move the ball forward 10 yards. If the offense fails to do this, the ball passes to the other side.

Imagine that the offense advances the ball by 4 yards on the first down. How many yards does it have to go?

$$10 - 4 = 6$$

6 yards?

But what if the defense pushes the offense back 7 yards? How many yards do they have to move forward after that?

$$10 + 7 = 17$$

17 yards!

A professional football team can have up to 53 players. On the other hand, only 11 of those players are allowed on the field at any time.

What we call soccer is known in most of the world as football, and our football is called American football.

The Longest Game

Officially, a football game is made up of 4 quarters lasting 15 minutes each. How long is that in total?

$$4 \times 15 = 60$$

60 minutes, or one hour!

But this total doesn't take time outs or overtime into account. Overtime is necessary if both teams have the same point total. In order to break the tie, they just have to keep playing. The longest game in NFL history took place in 1971 between the Kansas City Chiefs and the Miami Dolphins. It lasted 82 minutes. How much longer than a standard game is that?

$$82 - 60 = 22$$

22 minutes!

BASKETBALL

Basketball is another sport that, like football, uses a rectangular court. A regulation NBA basketball court is 94 feet long and 50 feet wide. At either end of the basketball court are baskets mounted onto a backboard precisely 10 feet off the ground.

Because the baskets themselves are high, most basketball players benefit from being very tall.

How tall are you? Imagine, for a moment, that you are four and a half feet tall. How much higher up is the basket on a basketball court?

$$10 - 4.5 = 5.5$$

The basket on a basketball court is about five and a half feet higher than you are! Now you understand why most basketball players are very tall!

If you watch a professional basketball game on television, you'll notice that each team has many players. This is mainly to allow for substitutions, though. The most players allowed on the court for either team is 5. These players cover the following positions:

1) Point guard
2) Shooting guard
3) Power forward
4) Small forward
5) Center

Assuming that both teams in a basketball game have as many players on the court as allowed, how many players in total are on the court?

$$5 + 5 = 10$$

10 players!

In comparison with baseball and football, basketball is a much quicker game. Both teams score points at a fast rate. This is partly why the point totals from a basketball game are so high, sometimes even going into triple-digit numbers.

*What is your average
total points per
basketball game?*

Here is a chart showing the ten all-time leaders for points per game:

Player	Total
Michael Jordan	30.1
Wilt Chamberlain	30.1
Elgin Baylor	27.4
Allen Iverson	27.2
Jerry West	27.0
Shaquille O'Neal	26.8
Bob Pettit	26.4
George Gervin	26.2
Oscar Robertson	25.7
Karl Malone	25.0

Something to bear in mind when looking at this chart is that the numbers in the Total column are averages. An **average** is a number that represents a group of numbers. In other words, Bob Pettit didn't earn 26.4 points for every game he played, but 26.4 is about the number of points he earned in most games.

Michael Jordan and Wilt Chamberlain are tied. But how many more points did they earn per game compared to George Gervin?

$$30.1 - 26.2 = 3.9$$

Compare Karl Malone and Shaquille O'Neal. Who earned more points per game and how many?

$$26.8 - 25.0 = 1.8$$

Shaquille O'Neal earned about 1.8 points more per game than Karl Malone!

What about this—we know that the numbers above are average totals for points per game for ten NBA players. Can you calculate the average total points per game for these ten players combined?

It's easy to do. First, add up all of the totals:

$$30.1 + 30.1 + 27.4 + 27.2 + 27.0 + 26.8 + 26.4 + 26.2 + 25.7 + 25.0 = 271.9$$

Next, divide the total by the number of **addends**. Addends are the numbers you added together. Since you already know that these are the numbers for the *top ten* all-time leaders in points per game, you know that there are 10 addends:

$$271.9 \div 10 = 27.19$$

The average score for the top ten leaders in points per game is 27.19!

Basketball Scoring

Each basket in a game of basketball can be worth anything from just 1 point up to 3 points. It all depends on where the basket was shot:

From behind the three-point line = 3 points

From inside the three-point line = 2 points

Foul shot = 1 point

So, if a player in a basketball game makes 7 baskets from inside the three-point line, 2 baskets from behind the three-point line, and 1 foul shot, how many points has he or she earned?

BOXING

Not all sports involve large teams of people or a great deal of equipment. One of the oldest sports in the world is also one of the simplest—boxing.

Boxing dates at least as far back as the culture of ancient Egypt, making it roughly 4,000 years old. Of course, the boxing we are familiar with today is very different from the boxing that was practiced by the Egyptians and later by the Greeks. For one thing, boxers in ancient times did not wear gloves. Another important difference is that modern boxing has weight categories.

You may already know something about weight classes even if you think that you don't. For instance, who is the most famous boxer in the world? Mike Tyson? Mike Tyson is famous for being the youngest person to ever win the *heavyweight* title.

Lightweight, **middleweight**, **heavyweight**…
These are all distinctions made to ensure
fairness. It wouldn't make much sense for a small
person to box a much larger person. The larger person
would have an unfair advantage. In order to prevent a
situation like this, boxers are categorized according to
how much they weigh. These categories are called
weight divisions.

According to the World Boxing Council, there are
seventeen weight divisions:

Strawweight – 105 pounds
Lightflyweight – 108 pounds
Flyweight – 112 pounds
Super Flyweight – 115 pounds
Bantamweight – 118 pounds
Superbantamweight – 122 pounds
Featherweight – 126 pounds
Superfeatherweight – 130 pounds
Lightweight – 135 pounds
Superlightweight – 140 pounds
Welterweight – 147 pounds
Superwelterweight – 154 pounds
Middleweight – 160 pounds
Supermiddleweight – 168 pounds
Lightheavyweight – 175 pounds
Cruiserweight – 200
Heavyweight – over 200 with no upper limit

The weights indicated here are the limits for each category. For instance, in order to qualify as a featherweight, a boxer can weigh anywhere between 123 and 126 pounds. Anything over that, though, would place the boxer in the next category, superfeatherweight.

Using the figures above, figure out how many more pounds a flyweight boxer weighs compared to a strawweight boxer.

To find out, just subtract the smaller number from the larger number:

$$112 - 105 = 7$$

A flyweight boxer weighs about 7 pounds more than a strawweight boxer!

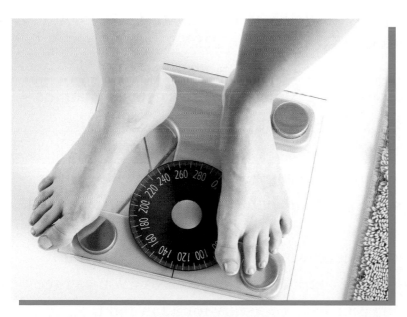

How much do you weigh? How much more would you need to weigh to qualify as a lightweight boxer? A heavyweight?

What about a lightweight boxer compared to a super flyweight boxer?

$$135 - 115 = 20$$

A lightweight boxer weighs about 20 pounds more than a super flyweight boxer!

Finally, you may have noticed that the *heaviest* category, the heavyweight division, has no upper weight limit. In other words, if you had two boxers with these weights:

315   225

They would both qualify as heavyweights! How many more pounds is 315 compared to 225?

$$315 - 225 = 90$$

The boxer weighing 315 is 90 pounds heavier than the boxer weighing 225! And yet they are both still in the heavyweight division!

Finally, compare a heavyweight boxer weighing 215 pounds to someone in the lightest category, a strawweight:

$$215 - 105 = 110$$

A 215-pound heavyweight boxer weighs about 110 pounds more than a strawweight boxer. Now you can see why weight divisions are necessary for a fair fight.

Track and field is one of the most popular Olympic events.

<u>The Olympics</u>

Baseball, basketball, and boxing are just some of the many games that make up the Olympics, a festival of sports that originated in Greece many hundreds of years ago. Other sports included in the Olympics include tennis, volleyball, and fencing.

The Olympics are held every 4 years. Here are the years in which the last Olympics were held:

1996
2000
2004

When will the next Olympic games be held?

NASCAR

Many of the sports we have been looking at are things you would not likely experience unless you wanted to do them. There is a sport, though, that almost everyone can relate to on some level, simply because it is such an essential part of life—driving.

NASCAR is actually an **acronym**, a word made up from the first letters in a group of words. NASCAR comes from the <u>N</u>ational <u>A</u>ssociation of <u>S</u>tock <u>C</u>ar <u>R</u>acing.

NASCAR has only been in existence for a little over 50 years, but since that time it has become an immensely popular sport. Crowds all over the country just can't get enough of the speeding, roaring cars.

In NASCAR a checkered flag means the race is finished.

Driving is something that almost everyone will experience at one point or another in life. The driving that NASCAR drivers do, though, is much different than the driving you see people do in your own neighborhood. NASCAR drivers race on specially paved tracks and at extremely high speeds.

Most of the time these speeds are well over 200 miles per hour. Let's compare that to the speed limit in a typical residential neighborhood, which is about 30 miles per hour.

$$200 \qquad 30$$

For one thing, you can subtract 30 from 200:

$$200 - 30 = 170$$

That gives you 170. So a NASCAR driver travels at an average speed roughly 170 miles per hour faster than a person driving through a residential neighborhood!

Another way to think about this, though, is to express the difference in terms of **multiples**. It might help you to think of the word multiples as being related to multiplication. You see, any number being multiplied produces multiples. For instance, multiply the number seven by some common **integers**:

$$0 \times 7 = 0$$
$$1 \times 7 = 7$$
$$2 \times 7 = 14$$

The answers 0, 7, and 14 are all multiples of 7!
Now consider these numbers:

$$5 \qquad 10$$

What would you have to multiply the number 5 by to give the **product** 10? You can find out by using division:

$$10 \div 5 = 2$$

Multiplying 5 by 2 gives 10. Another thing you can say here, though, is that the product 10 is *twice as much* as 5!

Let's apply this technique to the speeds of an everyday driver and a NASCAR driver:

$$200 \div 30 = 6.66$$

And just to keep things simple, round that number up to 7. Now you can say that a NASCAR driver drives at speeds about *seven times* as fast as an everyday driver!

Even in the fastest areas a regular car can only go about 75 miles per hour. How much slower is that than NASCAR drivers?

Since NASCAR is a **competitive** sport, there has to be some way for a driver's performance to be evaluated. This is done by a point system. Depending on when a driver finishes the race, he earns a specific number of points:

Place	Points
1st	180
2nd	170
3rd	165
4th	160
5th	155
6th	150
7th	146
8th	142
9th	138
10th	134
11th	130
12th	127
13th	124
14th	121
15th	118

...and so on until the last place driver, or 43rd, who receives only 34 points.

Imagine a race has just finished. How many more points does the 1st place driver receive compared to the 6th place driver?

$$180 - 150 = 30$$

The 1st place driver receives 30 more points than the 6th place driver!

How many more points does the 6th place driver receive compared to the 14th place driver?

$$150 - 121 = 29$$

The 6th place driver receives 29 more points than the 14th place driver!

Finally, compare the first and last place drivers. What kind of point **spread** lies between them?

$$180 - 34 = 146$$

The 1st place driver receives 146 more points than the 43rd place driver!

The Longest Track

The longest race in NASCAR is the Coca-Cola 600. 600 refers to the number of miles in the race. If a typical car in the Coca-Cola 600 is traveling at 200 miles per hour, how long will it take that car to complete a 600-mile distance?

$$600 \div 200 = 3$$

3 hours!

SKATEBOARDING

Just riding around on a skateboard without wiping out takes a lot of practice. That is why all the flashy tricks performed by professional skateboarders are so impressive. The ollie, the manual, and grinding all take fantastic coordination and skill.

Before it was known as skateboarding it was called "sidewalk surfing!"

Probably the most famous skateboarder of all time is Tony Hawk. One of Tony's biggest achievements came at the 1999 X Games when he became the first person ever to perform a stunt many thought was impossible. This stunt is called the 900. It took Hawk about 10 years of practice before he was able to do it successfully.

In a 900, a skater launches from a U-shaped skating ramp. While airborne, he rotates two and a half times. To understand why this trick is called a 900, you have to understand a bit about **circles** and **degrees**.

Degrees are a unit of measurement for circles developed by the ancient Greeks. A degree is basically a very small portion of a circle, like thin slices of a pie. Every circle can be divided into 360 degrees. It might help you to understand this concept better by looking closely at a compass. A compass is a circle marked with clearly labeled degrees. 0 degrees is the starting point of a circle. 360 degrees, on the other hand, is one complete revolution.

To perform a 900, a skateboarder has to rotate two and a half times. How many degrees is that?

First of all, find out how many degrees there are in two revolutions:

$$2 \times 360 = 720$$

There are 720 degrees in two revolutions!

Now you have to find out how many degrees there are in half a revolution. You already know that there are 360 degrees in one full revolution. You can find out how many degrees there are in half a revolution by dividing that amount by 2:

$$360 \div 2 = 180$$

There are 180 degrees in half a revolution!

To find out how many degrees there are in two and a half revolutions, you just have to add the results together:

$$720 + 180 = 900$$

There are 900 degrees in two and a half revolutions! Now you know where the trick gets its name!

Skate parks have built-in ramps that will help you practice and develop your own tricks.

Degrees are small portions of a circle, like extremely thin slices of pizza.

Longboards

Typical skateboards are about 31 inches long. Some skateboarders, though, decide that they want to go faster than a skateboard can travel. At that point, they can switch to something called a *longboard*.

The average longboard can be anywhere from 38 to 60 inches long.

If you have a longboard that is 45 inches long, how much longer is that than the average skateboard?

$$45 - 31 = 14$$

Fourteen inches longer!

CONCLUSION

What is your favorite sport? Maybe you have more than one. Certainly, there is a wide variety to choose from. If you don't like playing tennis you might like swimming. You might not like running, but maybe you enjoy skiing. Even people who don't actually play sports like to watch games and root for their favorite teams.

Even if you're not in a competitive sport, you can compete with yourself.

In this book we've mostly looked at competitive sports—sports that people play to earn points and win at something. There is another breed of sports, though, that has more to do with enjoyment and fun. These are called **recreational** sports. A recreational sport can be just about anything. Even recreational sports are full of math, though. How fast you go, how far you go, how long you do it. Numbers are what we use to measure all of these things. Sometimes, even if you're not competing with other people, you are in competition with yourself. Many runners, for instance, keep records to see how much they improve from week to week and month to month.

Did you know that there are even competitions where young people solve math problems? That means that not only is math a part of sports, it is a sport! Maybe you'll even want to try it for yourself!

If you really love sports, maybe you'll be a coach when you grow up!

THE METRIC SYSTEM

We actually have two systems of weights and measures in the United States. Quarts, pints, gallons, ounces, and pounds are all units of the U.S. Customary System, also known as the English System.

The other system of measurement, and the only one **sanctioned** by the United States Government, is the metric system, which is also known as the International System of Units. French scientists developed the metric system in the 1790s. The basic unit of measurement in the metric system is the **meter**, which is about one ten-millionth the distance from the North Pole to the equator.

A metal bar used to represent the length of the standard meter was even created. This bar was replaced in the 1980s, though, when scientists changed the standard of measurement for the meter to a portion of the distance traveled by light in a vacuum.

There are many, many sports to choose from.

The metric system can be applied to the world of sports in a number of different ways. Earlier, you learned that the distance from the pitcher's mound to home plate on a baseball field is 60.5 feet. What would that be in meters?

Converting feet to meters is simple. All you have to do is multiply the number of feet by 0.3:

$$60.5 \times 0.3 = 18.15$$

The distance from the pitcher's mound to home plate is about 18.15 meters!

Another area where the metric system can be applied to sports is speed. We know that most NASCAR drivers drive at speeds around 200 mph. In the metric system, though, speed is measured not in miles, but in kilometers. One mile is equal to 1.621 kilometers. How does a NASCAR driver travel in terms of kilometers? Since you already know the driver's speed in miles, you can find out by using multiplication:

$$200 \times 1.621 = 324.2$$

A NASCAR driver travels at about 324 kilometers per hour!

As you can see, the metric system is pretty easy once you get the hang of it. For practice, you could go through this book and convert some of the numbers to metric.

Try it!

GLOSSARY

acronym — a word made up from the first letters of other words

addends — the numbers added together in an addition problem

average — a number used to represent a group of numbers

circles — round objects

competitive — involving winning and losing

defense — the team trying to prevent the offense from scoring

degrees — small portions of a circle

heavyweight — a boxer who weighs 200 pounds or more

integers — numbers

lightweight — a boxer who weighs between 135 and 139 pounds

line of scrimmage — in football, the location on the field where play begins

meter — about 39.37 inches; one ten-millionth the distance from the North Pole to the equator

middleweight — a boxer who weighs between 160 and
    167 pounds

multiples — the result of multiplying a single number by
    a series of other numbers

offense — the team in possession of the ball

product — the result of multiplying two numbers

recreational — just for fun and enjoyment

sanctioned — allowed or encouraged

spread — the difference between winning and
    losing scores

Further Reading

Slavin, Steve. *All the Math You'll Ever Need.* John Wiley and Sons, Inc. 1999.

Zeman, Anne and Kate Kelly. *Everything You Need to Know About Math Homework.* Scholastic, 1994.

Zeman, Anne and Kate Kelly. *Everything You Need to Know About Science Homework.* Scholastic, 1994.

Websites to Visit

http://www.pbs.org/teachersource/mathline/concepts/sportsandmathematics.shtm
PBS TeacherSource – Sports and Mathematics

http://people.howstuffworks.com/baseball.htm
How Stuff Works – How Baseball Works

http://www.acdelco.com/html/nas_main.htm
NACAR Basics

INDEX

ABOUT THE AUTHOR

Kieran Walsh has written a variety of children's nonfiction books, primarily on historical and social studies topics, including the Rourke series *Holiday Celebrations* and *Countries in the News*. He lives in New York City.